HOW TO VISIT
POMPEII

GUIDE TO THE EXCAVATIONS
WITH A GENERAL PLAN

FALANGA EDIZIONI POMPEIANE

Text
PIEMME - Enrika D'Orta

FALANGA EDIZIONI POMPEIANE
Via Mazzini 1, Pompeii- phone 081/8598869

© Text by FEP
© Illustrations by CEB
Photos of the archives of
Casa Editrice Bonechi except for those on pages
1, 5, 7, 26, 35, 36, 38, 41, 45, 46, 48, 55, 79,
82, 84, 86 below, 87, 88 below, 89 below, 90, 91,
taken by Gianni dagli Orti

Printed in Italy by Centro Stampa Editoriale Bonechi,
1994

* * *

HOW TO VISIT THE ANCIENT CITY

This guide to the ruins of Pompeii describes and illustrates temples, houses, public buildings and roads of the ancient city.
The complete itinerary is marked on the map attached to the guide and is numbered consecutively from 1 to 89.
The complete visit, however, would take many hours, and so we have suggested three different itineries for those with less time at their disposal.

FIRST ITINERARY:
1-2-3-4-5-6-10-11-14-20-18-35-36-54-9

SECOND ITINERARY:
1-2-3-4-5-6-10-11-13-14-15-17-20-21-22-27-28-18-35-36-38-52-54-61-60-59-58

THIRD ITINERARY:
1-2-3-4-5-6-10-11-13-14-15-16-17-20-21-22-27-28-18-35-36-38-42-43-46-49-50-52-54-58-59-60-61-81-82-83-84-87-86

The bronze statue of the Faun.
On the opposite page, fresco of the widding between Mars
and Venus, on the first page, portrait of Mercury, both from the
House of Marcus Lucretius

HISTORICAL BACKGROUND

A hot sun shone down on 24 August 79 A.D., but the Pompeians, who were engrossed in their work and in the frantic life of the city, did not know that they had seen that wonderful sun for the last time. In the early hours of the afternoon, in fact, the summit of Vesuvius exploded with a frightening roar. A black river of ash and lapilli came out of the crater and ran through the city, leaving death and destruction in its wake. It was in this way that glorious Pompeii was buried under six or seven metres of earth.

During the 8th century B.C. some Oscans settled along the shore of the Tyrrhenian Sea founding a centre which was situated on an elevated lavic spur formed by an ancient eruption of Vesuvius. Pompeii's strategic position soon made it an object of great importance, first to the Etruscans. Then, in the 5th century, the Samnites arrived from the mountains of Irpinia, and put an end to the control the Greeks and Etruscans had over most of Campania. It was inevitable that Pompeii should come under the domination of Rome at the beginning of the Samnite Wars. It became a Roman colony in 80 B.C. and took the name of "Colonia Veneria Cornelia Pompeii", so refering both to her conquerer and to the goddess Venus, of whom he was particularly attached.

One thousand seven hundred years passed from that fatal 24th August before the architect Domenico Fontana, carryng out land improvements in the Sarno valley, had a tunnel built and came across some inscriptions by chance. Although the area of the excavation corresponded to the amphitheatre, no one suspected that they had discovered a buried city.

The first real exploration of a scientific nature took place in 1748, under the direction of Charles of Bourbon. It was in 1860 that Giuseppe Fiorelli invented the ingenious system of pouring liquid plaster into the spaces left in the bed of ashes. Almost miraculously people and events emerged; Pompeii returned to life.

Up to now about four fifths of Pompeii has been brought to light. This gives us a reasonably clear picture of how the city was built and organised. To the west there is the Forum, around which are grouped the temples and public buildings. In the foreground there is the Large Theatre and the rest is mainly occupied by houses. Outside the city gates is the necropolis. Pompeii used to be situated only 500 metres from the sea, but after the eruption of 79, when material was emptied into the gulf, the distance increased to two kilometres.

Pompeii was surrounded by a three kilometre long wall, in which there were eight gates.

The port of Pompeii was located on the coast. Although several buildings have been found, the exact location of the port has not been identified. The oldest buildings of Pompeii date back to the sixth century B.C. This urban area in all probability occupied only a small part of the south-western sector, between the main Forum and the Triangular Forum.

The city gradually expanded towards the north and east. Two centuries after the Romans established themselves, the Italians rebelled, and Pompeii, Stabia and Herculaneum joined the revolt. The Roman general Silla, however, reconquered the three cities. Stabia was destroyed and Pompeii became a Roman colony. Many of her inhabitants were forced to leave to make room for the new settlers.

Most of the ruins of Pompeii date back to the period after the establishment of the colony (80 B.C.).

The Forum was the political, economic and religious centre of the city. Grouped around it were the main temples, the buildings, the law courts, the Macellum and the Mensa Ponderaria.

It is difficult, however, to see how the city, which is a marvellous example of a rational urban system today, was originally. At the time of its destruction, in fact, the Forum was completely isolated from the surrounding area by a large arcade which encircled it on all sides, apart from the northern end, which was occupied by the Capitoline and two honorary arches. The roads of the city differed in width, but most of them were quite narrow. They were generally between 2.4 and 4.5 metres, the widest being a little more than 7 metres, and they were all paved with large, polygonal blocks made from the lava of Vesuvius.

Almost all the roads had pavements too, generally about 30 cms or more high.

Pompeii originally received its water supply from the River Sarno and from wells, but when the needs of the city increased, an aqueduct was built which carried water to all parts of the city. Large lead pipes ran under the pavements, carrying running water to the houses of the richest inhabitants, to the public baths and to the public fountains where the poorer people obtained their water.

The city of Pompeii had a density of 8,000-10,000 inhabitants. About 60% consisted of free men, and the remaining 40% were slaves. The slaves destined for the house came from the East. They were almost always well-educated, often more so than their owners. A small, prosperous family usually had two or three slaves; a larger one had many more, including those who were doctors or teachers. A slave could hope for freedom if it was granted him by his owner or by paying a large sum of money, in which case he became a "freedman".

Romans generally had three names, a praenomen (in front of the name), a name and a surname. Women used the feminine form of their father's name. Slaves had a single name, generally Greek. A "freedman" could add a second name using that of his ex-master and having his slave name as a surname.

House of the Vettii: decoration with fresco paintings

Urban Dwellings

Almost two-thirds of the urban area of Pompeii was taken up with private buildings, including houses, shops, offices and inns. The houses varied, according to the social status of the occupier:

1) The well-to-do class of the local aristocrats (land owners), and the middle-class consisting of business men, bankers, publicans, lawyers and orators (which was also the leading political class) lived in the more luxurious houses. They were in the "Italic" style, with the living-rooms around the atrium. Later, in the second century B.C., this basic style was enlarged with additions inspired by eastern Hellenistic architecture, with Greek names for the various rooms: peristyle (covered colonnade surrounding the garden), triclinium (dining-room), oecus (living area) and so on. In the south-western area, where there is a marked drop to the Sarno valley, the houses are interesting above all for their panoramic development on two or three terraces which corresponded to the natural slope of the land.

2) The more modest and less well-to-do class was that of the freedmen, poorer traders and craftsmen. They lived in smaller houses without a true atrium, but with the rooms gathered around a covered atrium (atrium testudinatum), a corridor (this type of house was called a "basilicale") or a xystus, a small court-yard with one, two or three porticos (a type of small peristyle) or a viridarium (enclosed garden). The decorations on the walls and floors were less luxurious, but there are still some elegant examples.

3) When the house and shop or office were in the same space, the dwelling consisted of some rooms behind the shop (retrobottega) or a mezzanine above the shop (pergula) reached by means of a wooden stairway. This "abitare in pergulis" was considered a particularly humble dwelling. The walls were rough or covered in coarse stuccowork, and the floors simply beaten or covered in "cocciopesto".
In general all types of houses were found together in all the various quarters, as is natural in a commercial and residential city.
Pompeii offers us, therefore, the unique possibility of studying private houses of all different types and their historical and social developments during a span of more than four centuries.
In the Samnite Age (fourth century B.C.), the house had a single atrium with no impluvium (pool used for collecting rain-water) with other rooms surrounding it. The next period before the Social Wars (Second century B.C., second

Samnite Age) was very important. It was during this time that the Samnites were influenced by the arrival of the Hellenes at the nearby port of Pozzuoli and began to build really elegant and imposing private houses.

Wall Decoration

This can be divided into four historical groups known as four styles. The First Style or Incrustation Style lasted until 80 B.C. and imitated the coloured marble facing. The Second Style or Architectural Style framed landscapes with architectural elements, creating an illusion of depth. The Third Style, which developed about the end of the first century B.C., abolished the prospective illusions but preserved a form of fantastic architectural decoration which was often used to frame small pictures. The Fourth Style was developed about the middle of the first century A.D. It was a very varied style. It was a repetition of the Third Style developing the fantastic, with the pictures becoming smaller and smaller or disappearing altogether, and the architectural elements becoming more and more fantastic and unreal.

The pictoral documentation at Pompeii confirms the dividing of artists into two groups, immaginary and mural. They were probably organized into groups formed by masters and assistants, or contractors with a group of workers, generally slaves or freedmen.

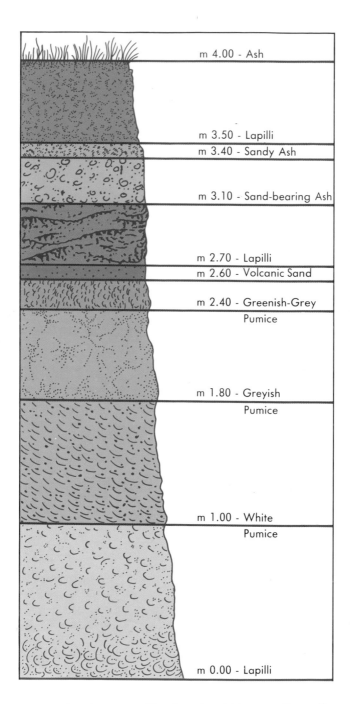

m 4.00 - Ash

m 3.50 - Lapilli

m 3.40 - Sandy Ash

m 3.10 - Sand-bearing Ash

m 2.70 - Lapilli

m 2.60 - Volcanic Sand

m 2.40 - Greenish-Grey
Pumice

m 1.80 - Greyish
Pumice

m 1.00 - White
Pumice

m 0.00 - Lapilli

Stratigraphical section of the deposits which cover Pompeii,
in the zone of the Large Palaestra

Two views of Vesuvius whose eruption of 24th August 79 A.D. caused the tragedy of Pompeii

Porta Marina

The Basilica

VISIT TO THE ARCHAEOLOGICAL EXCAVATIONS

1. PORTA MARINA
The entrance to the ruins is through Porta Marina, perhaps the most famous of the gates of the city, so called because it faces the sea. In more ancient times it was also called "Porta Neptunia", because near it there was a small temple dedicated to Neptune. It is composed of two openings, covered by a single vault: one was for pedestrians, the other, larger one, was for animals and vehicles.

2. ANTIQUARIUM
Much of the evidence of the life and civilization of Pompeii is to be found in the Antiquarium. It was found in 1861, destroyed by bombs in 1943 and finally rebuilt in 1948. It is composed of four rooms. The first two contain objects of the Samnite and Pre-Samnite Periods, mainly terracottas, Eutruscan pottery and sculptures in tuff. The third and fourth rooms, contain exhibits from Roman Pompeii, including the famous plaster casts of people and animals.

3. TEMPLE OF VENUS
As soon as you leave the Antiquarium, through a gate on the right, it is possible to see the site of the goddess of Venus, protectress of the city. Unfortunately, it was destroyed by the earthquake of 62 A.D. and completely ruined in 79 A.D. so we can see only a few remains of what was once a splendid temple.

4. BASILICA
We are without doubt in front of the most important public building in Pompeii. It was the seat of the law-courts and the centre of the economic life of the city. The Basilica opened onto the Eorum by means of five doorways which created three internal naves, the central one of which was formed by 28 brick columns, clearly of Greek influence. The date of the foundation of this Basilica is still uncertain and under discussion. It is thought, however, that it is from the pre-Roman age (about 120 B.C.), since some tiles found near the opening have the Oscan seal.

Temple of Apollo: on the opposite page, the bronze statue of the god; on this page, the ruins and the statue in the centre of the arcade

5. TEMPLE OF APOLLO

This temple was built in the third century B.C., and is formed of 48 Ionic columns, which were changed into Corinthian columns in Nero's age. On a high platform is the cella, the most sacred part of the temple, also surrounded by thirty Corinthian columns. There were several different deities in this temple, among them Apollo while shooting an arrow and opposite him, Diana the huntress. From other findings it is probable that Mercury was worshipped here too.

A general view of the Forum

6. THE FORUM

This rectangular square (32 metres wide and 142 metres long), paved in travertine and surrounded by a covered arcade on three sides, was the heart of political and religious life the city. During the Samnite age the arcade was composed of two orders of columns, built in Nocera tuff. These columns were in Doric style, whilst the trabeation

on which the upper columns rested was in Ionic style. The columns and trabeations on the eastern and western sides, however, are from the Roman period. At the centre of the western side of the square we can admire the "suggestum", which was the stand from which the orators spoke to the people. Along the southern side of the arcade are to be found several large bases on which were placed the

The Forum: the lefthand arcade

statues of the most important men of the city. The public buildings, which are to be found along the southern, eastern and western sides, were hidden by the colonnade, so that the only building completely visible was the Temple of Jupiter on the northern side, at the sides of which were two triumphal arches.

7. MUNICIPAL OFFICES

There are three public buildings which close the area south of the Forum. They are on a slightly higher level than the other buildings, are almost equal in size, and were almost certainly used by the city magistrates for administration. Owing to the importance of these buildings they were virtually rebuilt after the earthquake of 62 A.D., though still keeping their original form and size. Only the building to the east, next to Via delle Scuole, has its side and back walls in "opera incerta", which was used before 62 A.D.

8. ASSEMBLY ROOM

The building of the Assembly opens onto the south-eastern side of the Forum. Originally it was separated from the Forum and from Via dell'Abbondanza by a row of columns and therefore had many entrances on two sides. It is rightly supposed that the building is a "Comitium" where elections took place.

The many entrances and exits, five to the north and five to the west, allowed the voters to enter in an orderly manner from the Forum and to leave by Via dell'Abbondanza. On the southern side there is a tribune with stairs leading up to it, where the magistrates in charge of the elections were to be found. The walls of the Comitium were originally covered in marble, and the floor was also composed of marble slabs.

The municipal buildings on the southern side of the Forum

9. VIA DELL'ABBONDANZA

This elegant street stretches from the Forum to Porta di Sarno and takes its name from the beautiful fountain on which is sculptured in relief the symbol of Plenty: an opulent woman carrying a horn of plenty.

The road extends for 600 metres and in it we can relive life in the most commercial quarter of the prosperous city: all the most able devices and mature experiences of the past have been used to gather together elements and objects that would have otherwise been lost.

The roofs, with their tiles restored, have been replaced above the shops, and balconies and galleries jut out from the main parts of the houses. The doors, which had plaster casts taken of them from the holes left in the layers of ash, have again been decorated with their bronze door-knobs. Finally, in this street, which is one of the most important in the city, there is the most dramatic documentation of inscriptions painted on the walls.

Via dell'Abbondanza

The Building of Eumachia

10. THE BUILDING OF EUMACHIA

This building was the seat of the corporation of dyers and launderers, called "fullones". It was built at the expense of the priestess Eumachia and dedicated to Concordia Augusta (as can be read on the wooden joists above the door), another name for the Empress Livia, wife of Augusto. The entrance to the building is from the Forum. It has a double order of columns and a beautiful rectangular marble doorway, decorated with spirals of acanthus leaves. After the doorway there is a spacious court-yard at the back of which is a wall with three apses, the central one of which contains a statue of the Empress Livia. The statue of Eumachia was also situated in the court-yard, but today it is kept in the Archaeological Museum of Naples.

The Temple of Vespasian: the marble "ara" or altar with a basrelief depicting a sacrifice

11. THE TEMPLE OF VESPASIAN

The Temple of Vespasian, dedicated to the worship of the Emperor, is to be found along the eastern arcade, between the Building of Eumachia and the Sanctuary of the Lares.
The sculptured marble "ara" or altar, which depicts a scene of sacrifice, is very interesting. It is possible to recognize the sacrificing priest or "victimarius", the flag bearers, a flute-player and several assistants. The statue dedicated to this cult is to be found at the back of a tabernacle.

12. THE SANCTUARY OF THE LARES

This is certainly one of the most interesting and, in a certain sense, mysterious of the public buildings of Pompeii, due to its, complex architecture. It opens lengthways to the Forum. On a level with the arcade which surrounded the square there are eight quadrangular bases of basalt with traces of iron pivots for attaching slabs of marble.

They were probably bases for the columns of the arcade not yet rebuilt after the earthquake of 62 A.D. After the colonnade one enters a large, imposing atrium (18.20 by 19.90 metres). At the centre are the remains of an altar of which only the foundations are visible.

13. HORREA

Not far from the "Mensa Ponderaria" of the market (used to control the units of measure of the Roman system), there is a rectangular building whose front is formed by brick pillars. This is now used as a deposit for archaeological materials, but it was probably a "horrea", a shop selling special food-stuffs, possibly grain.

14. THE TEMPLE OF JUPITER

The temple closes the huge square of the Forum to the north and was built in the second century B.C., in the Samnite age. Dedicated to the trio Juno, Minerva and Jupiter, it had a pronaos or vestibule of twelve Corinthian columns, six at the front and three on each side. On the inside, the cella had a mixed floor composed of a marble mosaic. A marble head of Jupiter was found in the cella, and is now kept in the National Museum.

The Temple of Jupiter

To the left, one side of the Temple of Jupiter, in the centre, arch of Nero, to the right, the Macellum buildings

15. THE MACELLUM

The Macellum, or covered market, was built in the Imperial age, with an elegant entrance proceeded by a small portico of marble columns facing the Forum. Outside the square, shops were situated on the northern side, with small shops (or tabernae) on the inner southern side. At the centre of the uncovered area there is, as in other similar buildings, a circular dome-shaped construction (tholos) with a water basin. Towards the end of the building there is a tabernacle with two statues of members of the Imperial family, and on the right side, an area with a gutter for the water destined for the fish-market.

16. ARCH OF NERO

17. THE TEMPLE OF FORTUNA AUGUSTA

This temple was built in the year 3 A.D. by Marcus Tullius and dedicated to the Imperial cult. Access to the temple is by means of a flight of steps which reaches the `ara' and finally the vestible, decorated with six Corinthian columns. In the side walls there are two niches which contained statues, one of which was of Augustus.

The Temple of Fortuna Augusta

18. HOUSE OF THE FAUN

So-called because of the splendid bronze statue of the dancing Faun which decorates one of its impluvia. This can be justly considered the most beautiful example of a private house left to us from ancient times, because of its size, its architectural importance and its decorations.

It was probably built by Publius Silla, nephew of the dictator, who had the difficult job of organising the first installation of the Roman colony and of reconciling the interests of the original inhabitants and the new colonists. Apart from the dancing Faun, this house also provides the most incredible example of mosaic art: the huge mosaic of the Battle of Alexander the Great and other pictures, which are all in the National Museum of Naples. The building of this house took place at the height of the flowering of the Samnite civilization, and during the greatest period of influence of Hellenistic architecture. The architectural structure and decorations, in fact, show an admirable fusion of Italian and Hellenistic elements.

In front of the entrance is the greeting "Have". The entrance hall is furnished with double-doors and high up on the walls are two shrines for the Lares (the household

The House of the Faun

gods) in fine stucco-work. The floor is in `Opus sectile',
composed of pieces of coloured marble, like the basin of
the impluvium. The rear part of the house was developed
around two atria: the first is the main one, in Tuscan style,
following the traditional plan of Italian houses. The second, instead, is a tetrastyle atrium, with the roof resting on
four columns, as in the Hellenistic style. At the sides of the
tablinum of the main atrium were two triclinia (dining-
rooms) which, for the decorations on their mosaic floors
and above all for their orientation, must have been used in
autumn and in winter. At the rear of the two atria opens
the first peristyle with a covered arcade of 28 Ionic
columns, in the middle of which is the labrum (marble
support) of a fountain. On the walls can be seen the remains of precious decorations in stucco-work which admirably complete the architecture of the arcade. Precious
and luxurious was the exedra, which opens out from the
centre of the far wall of this peristyle. The entrance hall is
composed of imitation doors and columns decorated in

porphyry red stucco-work; the threshold is formed by a mosaic showing a landscapc of the Nile and the floor was a luxurious carpet stretched out in the form of the famous mosaic of the battle between Alexander the Great and Darius. To the sides of this exedra there are two summer: triclinia. A narrow corridor, stretching from the eastern side of the peristyle, was used to isolate the service area of kitchen, bathroom and stable.

The Statue of the Faun

Another view of the House of the Faun

The Arch of Caligola

19. ARCH OF CALIGOLA

The road which leads from the Forum to the northern walls of the city has a part ending with two arches. The one to the right of the temple of Jupiter is in honour of Nero Caesar. The other, which faced the main road of the city or so-called road of Fortuna, is dedicated to Caligola. His equestrian bronze was collected in fragments and is now in the Museum of Naples.

The Forum Baths

20. FORUM BATHS

At the cross-roads of Via del Foro and Via di Nola, we find the Forum Baths, excavated in 1823. They are divided into two sections, male and female, with a communal central-heating plant. After a short corridor there is the changing-room, with the small wooden cupboards for clothes and the seats where the customers could wait their turn. Leading off from the changing-room is the "frigidarium" at the centre of which is a circular tub for cold baths: an opening in the roof allows light to enter. To the right is the "tepidarium" (for warm baths) and the "calidarium" used for steam baths, which were heated by means of a system of double walls, called "concameratio", through which heat from the furnace passed. An elegant marble basin for washing reveals, in bronze lettering, the names of the magistrates who installed it in the baths at their expense, the price being 5,240 sesterces.

21. HOUSE OF THE TRAGIC POET

This house owes its name to a mosaic found in the tablinum, representing a carégo (an instructor of theatrical actors), and its notoriety to a series of beautiful frescoes showing heroic and mythical subjects like the famous Sacrifice of Iphigenia, which decorated the walls of the atrium and the peristyle (now in the Museum of Naples). It is perhaps the most typical house of the middle-class which began to prosper during the last years of Pompeii. Two shops at the sides of the door, in communication with the vestibule show that the owner of this elegant dwelling was also a merchant. On the floor of the entrance hall is the mosaic of a dog attached to a chain, with the motto "cave canem" (beware of the dog). Around the small atrium with its marble basin are the various rooms of the ground floor. A tablinum is decorated with a picture showing Admeto and Alcesti and with a theatrical mosaic.

At the rear of the building is the Lararium, in the form of a small temple. After a narrow, rustic kitchen, there is a large triclinium, with pictures of Venus contemplating a nest of Cupids, of Ariadne abandoned and the myth of Diana. To the left of the peristyle are two other rooms with small pictures showing Ariadne and Theseus, Venus the Fisherwoman and Narcissus at the fountain. In the north-west corner there is a second entrance to the house leading onto the Strada della Fullonica.

22. HOUSE OF PANSA

Built in the Samnite age, this is an enormous house which was divided into various small apartments to rent, with separate entrances, by its last owner. Nothing remains of

its original decoration, but the beautiful peristyle still ex-
ists, surrounding a large pool instead of a garden as was
more usual.

23. BAKERY

This was an older house, later changed to be used as a
bakery. The western half remained dwelling, with four
strong brick pillars at the corners of the impluvium to raise
the rooms above which were used as living quarters. In the
eastern half, the garden was transformed into a pistrinum
or bread bakery, with stone mills for milling, an oven for
baking, a horrea for storing the grain, a stable for the animals used to turn the mill and finally, a shop for selling the
finished product.

24. HOUSE OF SALLUST

To be considered one of the noblest examples of pre-
Roman dwellings of the Samnite age. The large Tuscan
atrium with the basin for the impluvium, the characteristic
doors with their tapering openings, and the walls of the
airy tablinum, of the oecus facing the covered arcade and
of one the cubicles, still preserve most of the decoration in
the First style, with the covering in stucco-work imitating
the incrustation of polycrome marble with its reliefs and
colours. Of a completely different character is the small
peristyle with hexagonal columns to the southern side
which show us, with the different proportions and purposes of the rooms, the style of decoration used in Pompeii
during the post-Augustan age. On one of the walls was
painted a landscape, Actaeon surprising Ariadne in her
bath, unfortunately destroyed during World War II.

The House of Sallust

25. HOUSE OF THE SURGEON

The massive, severe façade of large blocks of limestone and the internal positioning of the rooms makes this the most typical and best preserved example of a house of the Calcareous age (IV-III century B.C.) derived from the oldest scheme of the Italian house. The changes which took place have not altered its primitive character. A precious series of surgical instruments was found in this house, which constitutes one of the most important pieces of evidence of ancient surgery. They are now kept in the Museum of Naples.

26. VIA DEI SEPOLCRI (OR OF THE TOMBS)

Although the tombs brought to light outside Porta Nocera are doubtlessly of historical and architectural interest, the most famous and most complete necroplis of Pompeii, connected to the first discoveries of the city, is that outside Porta Ercolano. It is to be found in the northern suburb and is known as "Via dei Sepolcri".

27. HOUSE OF THE SMALL FOUNTAIN

On the walls of the pretty nymphaeum there is a large landscape showing seaside and country houses.

28. HOUSE OF THE LARGE FOUNTAIN

This house takes its name from the large fountain which adorns it. The fountain is in a niche, and is typically eastern, coming from Egypt at the time of the Roman conquest. The decoration of the niche consists of a beautiful mosaic, bringing to mind the magnificence of oriental carpets. A type of glass-paste was used for the mosaic work.

A view of Via dei Sepolcri which leads to the Villa of the Mysteries

The Large Fountain

The subjects of this tasteful and patient work are for the most part birds, arabesques and geometric designs. Water flowed out of the mouth of a statue representing a marine goddess. At the sides of the fountain are two marble theatrical masks and, at the bottom, a bronze cupid with a dolphin on his shoulder.

29. HOUSE OF CASTOR AND POLLUX

This house is situated around one of the four Corinthian-type atria preserved in Pompeii, the atrium here being of twelve tuff columns. The wall decorations were executed by the same hands as those of the house of the Vetti. The most important pictures have been transferred to the National Museum of Naples. The peristyle, however, which was added to the original nucleus of the house, still has some excellent pictures: they are panels between thin architectural beams with still-lives inserted.

30. HOUSE OF THE CENTAUR

The house of the Centaur is composed of three houses converted into one and has, to the right of the entrance, a beautiful cubicula decorated in the First Style. Beyond this is the House of Castor and Pollux, also obtained from the union of three older houses, partly recognizable, the union of which did not take place before the Augustan age. The atrium of the House of the Centaur, corresponding to the main entrance, is one of the most magnificent examples of a Corinthian atrium with twelve columns. In the room to the right of the tablinum there are the following pictures: Birth of Adonis, and Scylla giving Minos the magic hat of his father. In the left-hand room there is: Apollo and Daphne, and Silenus with Nymph and the Infant Bacchus. Behind the tablinum there is a handsome portico with Doric columns and at the rear, the shrine of the Lares. To the right of the atrium there is a second peristyle with a large pool of water in the centre. It is not so elegant and airy as that of the House of Meleager, but the walls are still decorated, for the most part, in the Fourth Style: frames filled in with panels displaying richly ornamental elements and fantastic architecture.

A walled-up barrel in Via dell'Abbondanza

31. HOUSE OF APOLLO

The fact that Apollo appears several times in the pictures of this house has given it its name.

The entrance to the tablinum is flanked by two marble-covered bases, one for a small statue of Apollo and the other for a young Faun running after a servent. The painting still visible in the tablinum offers an example of panels hanging between slender architectural elements, like in the house of the Vetti. A small picture of Venus looking in a mirror is flanked by two medallions again showing Venus with a Cupid on her shoulder. In the viridarium (Roman garden), at the back, there is a fountain in the shape of a pyramid with marble steps and ornamental statues which is connected to the picture of a garden which does not exist anymore. Three steps to the right lead down to the lower part of the garden which extends to the urban wall and is surrounded on three sides by an elevated embankment used for the cultivation of plants and flowers. At the centre there is the round basin of a fountain, and against the back wall, a summer triclinium, protected by a sloping roof and supported by four columns. The outer wall of the cubicola, at the back of the garden to the left, gives us some idea of the sumptuous decoration, with its rustic covering consisting of fragments of limestone from Sarno, and a coloured mosaic picture. The picture shows Achilles, disguised and hidden among the children of King Licomede of Scyros, where he had found refuge in order to escape taking part in the Trojan War, being recognized by Ulysses.

One of the daughters, Deidamia, terrified, is also present. Another two mosaics, one of Achilles unsheathing his sword against Agamemnon to gain possession of Briseide, and the other of the three Graces, also to be found on the walls in the garden, were removed and taken to the National Museum of Naples. Another marvellous picture is that showing the "musical competition between Apollo and Marsyas", painted in the Fourth Style.

32. TOWER OF MERCURY

The "Vicolo di Mercurio" is closed at the far end by one of the towers of the fortifications (tenth tower), which represents the last phase of construction just proceeding the siege and conquest by Silla (89 B.C.). Examinations which have taken place in the last few years, after removing part of the ancient embankment, show clearly that the tower was built in a gap in the walls, superimposed on one of the gates of the walls. From the city walls it is possible to see the internal walls, composed of tuff pillars in limestone, marked by letters and symbols of the Oscan alphabet. The partly restored tower offers, from its upper terrace, a superb view of the ruins of the once-buried city, closed in by Vesuvius, the Latteri Mountains and the sea.

33. HOUSE OF THE MELEAGER

An elegant house of the Samnite age, it is decorated, however, in the Fourth Style. Architecturally magnificent is the peristyle, which opens out from one of the sides of the house. There is a colonnade which surrounds a large garden pool, with a fountain and statuettes. On the eastern side there are three rooms, the centre one with the layout of a large, luxurious reception-room, that is with an internal colonnade in the Hellenistic style, known as "oecus corinthius". In the north-eastern corner there is another triclinum, whose elegant decoration is badly preserved.

34. HOUSE OF THE LABYRINTH

This is also an imposing house of the Samnite period, with a double atrium: that is, with a main atrium (tetrastyle) and a second, Tuscan atrium. Above all noteworthy, is the group of rooms used as luxurious reception rooms. The central room which, with its internal colonnade (oecus corinthius) is like that of the House of Meleager, and the nearby cubicle, both contain the most beautiful examples of pictorial decorations of the Second Style, with architectural motives and designs. The adjoining room is inlaid with a picture in mosaic of the myth of Theseus and the Minotaur in the Labyrinth. The part of the house to the west is rather rustic in style, containing, apart from ovens and mills, a private bath.

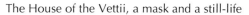

The House of the Vettii, a mask and a still-life

35. HOUSE OF THE VETTII

This is the house which best shows the wealth of the merchants in the last ten years of the city's life. This wealth is shown in the luxurious wall decorations and in the striking layout of the garden. The two owners, Aulo Vettio Restituto and Aulo Vettio Conviva were doubtlessly newly rich merchants, but it is impossible to guess their trade or the origins of their wealth from the house, since it contains no shops or businesses. The outside of the building already shows characteristics of comfort and wealth: the two secondary façades, facing the southern and eastern streets, are entirely covered in "cocciopesto", and the bases of the walls protected by a large border of masonry and "cocciopesto" all around, covering most of the narrow pavement, so protecting the inside from humidity. From the entrance hall the inside of the house is immediately intimate and deeply suggestive: due to the restoration of the roofs, necessary for the protection of the paintings, we can finally see the inside of a Pompeian house with its shadows and lights and its sense of a family dwelling. The plan can be considered divided into two parts: the main part of the house is to be found around the main atrium and the peri-

The House of the Vettii: the altar of the Lares

The House of the Vettii

style, while the more rustic quarter consisting of the servants' rooms, the kitchen and the upper rooms, is around the secondary atrium to the north-east. The essential value of this dwelling is the rich and complete wall decorations which are almost unique in their miraculous survival. In two centuries of excavations many houses have been uncovered but this one alone can be considered a rare, ancient picture gallery.

The are pictures in the Fourth Style, ornamental, full of fantastic architecture with a rich variety of decorative elements, enlightened by pictures showing mythical and heroic subjects and enlivened by friezes and areas of exquisite miniature art. The decorations are all of the same period (except for a few areas), although painted by different artists; that is, after the earthquake of 62 A.D., which badly damaged the building and some of the pictures in the house.

Passing through the vestibule we can see an obscene picture of Priapus resting his enormous phallus on one side of a pair of scales. This figure was placed at the entrance to the house to ward off the evil eye of those jealous of the wealth of the Vettiis. The atrium has had its roof restored

The House of the Vettii: detail of the fresco depicting Daedalus and Pasiphae

which has reduced its size and also the light available: at the sides are two strongboxes (orcae). In the room to the left of the entrance hall, under a frieze of fish in a pond, there are two small pictures of little value: Ariadne deserted and Hero and Leander. In the larger room, with a low, flat ceiling, there are the following pictures: Cyparissus, in despair after having mistakenly killed a favourite deer, being changed into a cypress tree; Pan and Cupid fighting; Jupiter enthroned and Leda and Danae. Two cubicles and two wings open off from the atrium. In the wing to the left there are panels showing a scene of fighting cocks, whilst in the wing to the right there are small medallions showing the heads of Medusa and Silenus, with vigorous and expressive faces.

From the atrium one passes, without the intermediate tablinum, into the beautiful peristyle with the garden. The many marble and bronze statues are satyrs and putti (Cupids) and are all fountain statuettes; the water passed through lead pipes, filled the pools and sprayed out of the fountains, forming magnificent water displays. The triclinium is in the main part of the covered arcade and from it there is a magnificent view of this beautiful garden. Not to

The House of the Vettii: Priapus weighing his phallus

The House of the Vettii: Hercules strangling snakes

be missed is the decoration of this luxurious triclinium. The red background of the walls is divided by large black pillars which seem to copy the arches of a loggia nearby because of the curves on the upper parts of the pillars. The pictures which occupied the central square of each wall were probably painted on wood and have been destroyed. Most of the decoration of the lower part of the wall, in the miniature style, still remains, however. On the cornice bordering the plinth there is a series of scenes of Cupids performing and selling flowers; Cupids preparing and selling oils and perfumes; a chariot race; Cupid goldsmiths and metal-workers; Cupids washing and dyeing; Cupids gathering grapes; the triumph of Bacchus and Cupids at a wine market. Beneath, near the pillars are panels with groups of Psyches and finally, in the central squares of the long walls are panels with mythological subjects. On the right-hand wall: Agamemnon about to kill the deer sacred to Artemis and Apollo slaying the python. On the left-hand wall Orestes and Pylades in front of 58 rhoas and Iphigenia.

The House of the Vettii: Apollo slaying the python

In the red side panels there are romantic couples from myths and legends; Perseus and Andromeda, Dionysius and Ariadne, Apollo and Diana and Poseidon and Amymone.

In one of the rooms to the north-east there is a plinth with imitation marble, three paintings at the centre of the walls, groups of Bacchants, mock architecture and panels containing seascapes. Towards the top of the walls there is a richly decorated frieze where figures of divinities alternate with fantastic architecture. In the pictures from the left are: Daedalus presenting Pasiphae the wooden cow; Ixion tied to the wheel of Hephaestus watched by an angry Juno, with Nephele, Ixion's lover, at the foot of the throne in anguish. To the right is Dionysus suprising the sleeping Ariadne. In the other smaller room to the south-east, the pictures and the architectural prospects stand out on the walls and here represent three myths of the Theban cycle: the infant Hercules strangling a serpent sent by Juno, Pentheus being killed by the enraged bull, the subject which, in the famous "Toro Farnese" is translated into the

The House of the Vettii: Cupids with wine amphorae

largest group statue that has been handed down from ancient times.
Next to the triclinium is a small, pretty portico which illu-
minates the rooms of an appartment reserved for the
women of the house (gineceo). Finally, in the secondary
atrium, to the west, there is a beautiful lararium or small
temple, decorated in stucco-work, with the figure of a
Genus or head of the family, between the Lares: underneath there is the snake Agathodemone with funeral offerings. In a small courtyard in a hidden part of the house is
the kitchen: on the ashes of the hearth there are still a triv-
et and a cauldron in bronze. Next to it is the kitchen sink.

The House of the Vettii: Cupids

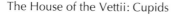

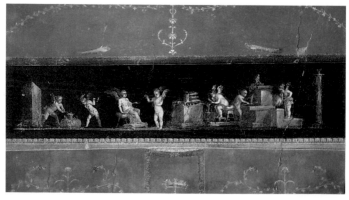

The House of the Golden Cupids

36. HOUSE OF THE GOLDEN CUPIDS

Despite the modest entrance and atrium, this house was one of the most beautiful in Pompeii, not for its size, but for the magnificent internal walls. From certain graffiti found it is assumed that it belonged to the family Poppaeus, a rich Pompeian family possibily related to Nero through Poppaea. In the two cubicles to the sides of the entrance there is still the decoration in the First Style, including the jutting out cornice, left in place when the walls were painted again. These rooms were without a doubt for the servants.

On the threshold of the tablinum, which has its wall painting and floor mosaic almost intact, there is a series of paintings, the central ones showing a libatory vase.

From the peristyle, with its floor of "cocciopesto", decorated with white and coloured tiles, one enters, to the left, an entertainment room with a large rose mosaic at the centre. The wall paintings are of the Third Style, and show: Acchiles between Briseis and Patroclus in the tent; Thesis visiting the workshop of Vulcan to buy new weapons for his son Achilles; and Jason in front of Pelias before fleeing with Medea.

From here it is possible to see the well-kept garden between the columns, with its flower-beds, hermae (small sculptures on columns) and marble tables sculptured with

43

Dionysian subjects. These include miniatures to be found around the central pool which is covered in stucco-work, and along which is a series of small sculptured animals: a wild boar attacked by a dog which is biting its right ear and a dog tearing a bird to pieces, all facing the direction of the pool.

Altogether it gives the impression of good taste and the masks, hung between the columns, and the "oscilla" (marble discs swinging in the wind to ward off the evil-eye) add to this impression. At the centre of the western arcade there is a large triclinium with two smaller side rooms. In the right-hand one are mural paintings showing: Diana and Actaeon, Leda and Venus as a Fisherwoman. In the southern arcade, next to a large decorated room, we find the cubicle with the famous "gilded Cupids" from which the house takes its name.

37. PORTA VESUVIUS

One of the main gates of the city, it was badly damaged in the earthquake of 62 A.D., and when the catastrophe of 79 A.D. occurred it was being rebuilt.

Along the eastern embankment there is a section of the city fortifications which is pre-Samnite. Next to this gate is the "Castellum Aquae" which divided the water which flowed from part of the Augustan aqueduct of Serino, and which was deviated in three directions.

38. HOUSE OF THE SILVER WEDDING

Excavated in 1893 when the sovereigns of Italy celebrated their Silver Wedding Anniversary, this house was called "Silver Wedding" in their honour.

The beautiful patrician dwelling dates from the Samnite age but was renovated both in structure and decoration in the Imperial age.

From the atrium, one passes to the peristyle, the most luxurious part of which is to the south. To the left there is a room decorated in the Second Style, supported by four columms too.

An exedra, to be found along the "ambulacro" has a magnificent yellow background, decorated with festoons. Finally, there is also the area of the private bath, "tepida rium" and "calidarium", while the "frigidarium" in outside in the garden.

39. GAMBLING HOUSE

This building, with its beautiful reticular façade and with the emblem of a vase (fritillum) between two phalluses, was one of the most important gambling houses in the city. Both young men and women frequented it and the owner noted on the walls the profits he made from the hospitality offered to couples in the bedrooms he had on the upper floor.

The House of the Silver Wedding: a frescoed room

40. HOUSE OF LUCIUS CAECILIUS JUCUNDUS

Right opposite the House of Orpheus, at No. 26, we find the House of Lucius Caecilius Jucundus, noted by the experts not only for its beauty, but above all for the information given on banking systems. During excavations, in fact, a strong-box was found, inside which were wax tablets of bankers' receipts, perfectly preserved and an exceptional bronze bust of the owner of the house, certainly an expert banker; Caecilius Jucundus enjoyed having a beautiful house. In the atrium, to the left, are handsome marble reliefs of the Chapel of the Lares. They have a votive character: one represents the Temple of Jupiter and the Triumphal Arch of the Forum while the other shows Porta Vesuvius with the "tripartitore" of water that collapsed during the earthquake (62 A.D.). The herma next to the tablinum was used to support the bronze statue of the owner of the house. This bust was erected by a faithful slave who was freed by Caecilius Jucundus. In the tablinum there is a beautiful decoration in the Third Style, unfortunately badly damaged.

45

41. HOUSE OF ORPHEUS

The portrait in the atrium (now in the Antiquarium) offered by the treasurer Anteros Arcarius, was dedicated to Primus. The surname of the owner, integrated with the name of Vesonis, is to be found in an electoral inscription on the wall of the nearby Fullonica, of which he was manager. There is a large picture of Orpheus among the wild beasts at the rear of the garden.

The cubicle behind, with its yellow background, is an example of late Third Style. It was in this room that the chained dog, whose plaster cast is in the Antiquarium, was found.

42. HOUSE OF MARCUS LUCRETIUS FRONTO

The House of Marcus Lucretius Fronto, who was a member of one of the most important families to settle in Pompeii in the Augustan age, is modest in size, but with very refined decoration in the Third Style (35-45 A.D.). Immediately after the vestibulum is the Tuscan atrium,

The House of Marcus Lucretius Fronto: a fresco of Narcissus at the fountain

delicately painted black; the floor is of crushed lava covered with small pieces of marble. The walls are black, revived by vertical stripes of yellow with arabesques and small hunting scenes at the centres of the panels. The border of the impuvium, in mosaic with a plaited design in black and white, dates back from the time of the installment of a new marble impluvium, with moulded borders.

To the right of the tablinum are other beautifully executed paintings. To the right of the atrium, instead, are frescoes representing the Toilet of Venus and Theseus and Ariadne. There are also mural decorations in the triclinium. At the back of the house is a raised garden with a summer triclinium on whose walls is a typical African landscape.

43. HOUSE OF THE GLADIATORS

The picture of the battle in the Amphitheatre between the men of Pompeii and Nocera (removed and now in the National Museum of Naples), of great historical interest, was found on the right-hand wall of the peristyle. In order to complete this picture the painter was compelled to partly destroy an older decoration of athletic games. Two other small pictures with gladiators' cups, also on new plaster, have now been destroyed.

44. PORTA DI NOLA

Porta di Nola is at the east end of the main street of Pompeii. For the most part it is built of tuff, except for part of the external walls, outside the city, which are in limestone and cover a tuff building in the guise of a rampart, flanking both sides of the entrance to the city. The building method used for this gate was simple and practical, especially when forecasting an enemy attack.

The actual gate is proceeded outside the city by two walls with spaces between them, ending with the two forementioned ramparts, which are connected to the fortified perimetrical wall. Before reaching the gate, therefore, the enemy had to overcome a narrow, unprotected gorge which was very dangerous for them.

The double spaces to the sides, which had several internal buttresses, had stairways to the wall. Steps have, in fact, been found on both sides of the gate. The keystone of the façade facing the city is decorated with a head of Minerva, in tuff, following a tradition of the Italic world and born, perhaps, of the need to place the gate of the city under the direct protection of the gods.

45. HOUSE OF OBELIUS FIRMUS

This was a house with a double atrium, built of large limestone blocks, inserted into the tops of the walls to contain the lava and limestone stones used to fill in the gaps.

The impressively well-built structure dates from the

Samnite age, when houses were mainly built of lava and limestone, without the addition of tuff. Here tuff appears in the columns and in the impluvia of the atria and peristyle.

The external view of the house was rather austere, the windows being high up and the façade closed. The internal flooring is simple, beaten lava with small pieces of white stone, without mosaics.

On the shorter rear side of the impluvium is the usual succession of cartibulum (table for plates), pedestal and table. In the corner, to the right of the atrium is the lararium and, as a sign of wealth, there is still the bronze strong-box, irremovable, in the wing to the right of the atrium. The secondary, Tuscan atrium, which is in communication with the main one through two rooms with two exits, has a similar layout but is smaller. Here, however the fauces are longer, due to the two shops next to it.

46. HOUSE OF THE CENTENNIAL

This house was built during the period of tuff (second century B.C.) with a double Tuscan atrium and an almost square peristyle of double ordered columns in the rear wing. About the beginning of the first century A.D., the

The House of the Centennial: fresco with erotic subject

house was remodernized and redecorated with black and white mosaics and pictures of the Third Style, begun, according to a graffito, about 15 A.D. At the same time, a bathroom and a swimming-pool were installed.

The final rooms to be transformed were the white room and the black room to the sides of the tablinum, a cubicle to be found in the eastern part of the house, with two good quality paintings of erotic scenes. An attractive painting of Vesuvius, wooded and covered in grapevines, from the lararium of the secondary atrium, also dates from this period (now in the Museum of Naples). The servants' quarters had a separate entrance, leading onto the street to the west of the house.

47. CENTRAL BATHS

The position of these baths, which were to become the most important in Pompeii, clearly show that the economic and commercial centre of the city was gradually moving from the Forum towards Via Stabiana.

The Central Baths, begun after 62 A.D. and occupying a whole block are, in fact, to be found at the cross-roads of Via di Nola and Via Stabiana. It seems clear that the magistrates intended to furnish the large residential area to the north-east with a modern baths complex, capable of meeting their needs. The building was never finished. On the southern side of the baths, on the other side of Vicolo di Tesmo, the houses are still in ruins. It is thought that perhaps they wanted to leave an area to remind them of the last Pompeian building phase.

The whole of the external perimeter is constructed in "opera incerta", using materials taken from demolished houses. The internal nucleus of the building, instead, shows different types of structural systems, used to brighten up the walls with their colours. The external eastern side is in "opera laterizia". The southern side, corresponding to the "calidarium" but on the courtyard, has a skirting board in mixed "opera incerta" with brick. The walls, from the level of the windows upwards, are in brick.

The main façade to the west, facing the palaestra, with its large windows, is in "opera incerta" with panels of "opera reticolata".

The main entrance is from Via di Nola. To the left of the entrance are two small rooms, the first of which was probably used as a ticket office and the second perhaps for depositing valuables, guarded by a "capsarius" (attendant). Behind the two rooms is a stairway which led to the upper floor. In these baths there was no "frigidarium" (for cold water bathing), evidently considered useless. From the "apodyterium", one passes, by means of the doors, to the "tepidarium" (for warm water bathing), illuminated by three windows.

The room had internal central heating with hot air passing both under the floors and through the walls, using the system of double walls. A narrow passage on the eastern side led to the "laconicum" (a very hot room used for sweating). This was a dome-shaped room with curved walls and four corner apses. Three small windows in the vault brought light into the room. This "laconium" was used for hot, dry baths. This explains its position, between the "tepidarium" and also its system of heating.

From the "tepidarium" one passes into the "calidarium", the most beautiful room of the baths, with its walls containing a series of quadrangular and semi-circular niches. In its finished state it would probably have been decorated with statues and stucco-work.

The "calidarium" is also well-lit: five windows can be found in the niches on the eastern side and three large windows, under which there is the bath for hot water bathing, face the palaestra.

Another bath for hot water bathing is on the opposite side. The baths were never completed, however. Among other things there is no praefurnium; with the furnaces for the heating of the water. The central baths are exclusively masculine.

48. HOUSE OF MARCUS LUCRETIUS

The atrium of this house seems to have been covered by a roof for which reason there is no impluvium. The name of the presumed owner is taken from a painting in a room to the left of the garden, which shows a writing-case and a letter addressed to Marcus Lucretius, priest of Mars and decurion of the city.

The water from the mosaic fountain to the rear of the garden came out of a marble statue of Silenus. The statue is more or less intact, including the taps.

49. BAKERIES AND MILLS

The mills were composed of two parts made out of volcanic rock, with a base to hold them. The lower stone (meta) was conical in shape and acted as a rotation axis while the upper one was hollow at the top, and biconical (catillus).

Using a wooden framework with two jutting arms it was turned either by men or mules. These mills took up the whole area of the floor of the mill. The grain was poured slowly into the cavity of the catillus, crushed between the surfaces of the two stones and collected as flour around the circular stone base which was protected by a thin sheet of lead.

The presence of the counters for kneading the dough, the ovens and the shops for selling all next to the mills, show that the bread industry was still primitive in ancient times.

The Bakery of Modesto

50. BAKERY OF MODESTO

The bakery of Modesto is very interesting with its mills composed of two pieces of volcanic rock, the lower one in the form of a cone and the upper one, hollow and biconical in shape. At the top there was the rotation axis which ground the grain by means of a special wooden clamp with two jutting arms.

The mills were turned by slaves, convicts serving life imprisonment or mules.

Beside the oven was the base of a container which originally held water to dampen the half-baked bread in order to obtain a shiny crust, and to cool the shovel. Wood was used to heat the ovens. A layer of sand underneath the floor of the oven and on top of the cover prevented heat loss. The opening of the oven was often made of slabs of lava which was more resistant, and it was closed with an iron door. The oven of the bakery was surmounted by a sheet of travertine on which there was a phallus in relief with the inscription: hic habitat felicitas (it is here that happiness lives). This sign is now in private room of the Museum of Naples.

In the Bakery of Modesto, behind the closed doors, eighty-one carbonized loaves were found. The room to the left of the oven was used for storing the finished product, and next to it was perhaps the "horreum" or granary.

The Brothel

51. HOUSE OF THE BEAR
In the mosaic floor of the vestibulum (entrance), underneath a greeting to those who enter (have), there is a wounded bear, from which the house takes its name.

52. THE BROTHEL
As with almost all brothels, this one also occupies an intersection between two secondary roads. It was an establishment with ten beds, five of which were on the upper floor, reached by means of a wooden stairway.

The Brothel: interior

The Brothel: an erotic scene

It was here that an uneaten plate of pasta and beans was found.A projecting gallery, with windows, allowed free movement in front of the rooms on the upper flooor which was more spacious. On the ground floor there were two entrances (at Nos. 18 and 19) and five rooms, each with a bed built into the wall and a wooden door. The tops of the beds, although they were covered by a short mattress, still show the marks left by the shoes of the visitors. On the walls of the rooms are painted scenes of the erotic games which could take place at the request of the clients. Next to these scenes, to the right of the main entrance is the figure of Priapus with two phalluses. He is holding his phalluses in his hands, and is standing near a fig tree.

53. INN OF SITTIUS
Even though it contained two entrances, this "hospitium" must have been rather small, since its triclinium could hold only nine people. The owner of the inn was certainly Sittius, a descendent of Sittio Nucerino Veterano, a member of Caesar's army in the civil wars in Apice.

54. STABIAN BATHS
These are without a doubt the oldest baths in Pompeii. Several different building stages can be distinguished, the first phase probably taking place about the fourth century B.C. The famous trapezoidal courtyard of the palaestra probably dates from this period. The Stabian Baths take their name from Via di Stabia which runs along the eastern side.

An interior of the Stabian Baths and the great courtyard

55. HOUSE OF CORNELIUS RUFUS

This is a noble house of the Cornelia Family. They probably came to Pompeii around the time of the colonization by Silla. The herma (bust) of the owner, with inscription, leaned against one of the doors of the tablinum. The superb marble impluvium in the atrium, and the two beautiful trapezophorons (supports for the marble table), excellenty decorated, are to be admired.

56. TEMPLE OF ISIS

Dating from the pre-Roman age, this temple was almost entirely rebuilt after the earthquake of 62 A.D., at the expense of Popidius Celsinus, and is the best-preserved temple of the city. According to the inscriptrion on the architrave above the entrance door, the aforementioned Popidius Celsinus was elected decurion, even though he was only six years old. The structure and the decorations of the furnishings came to light perfectly preserved, but the sacred objects of the cult, sculptures and paintings have been taken to the National Museum of Naples.

The sanctuary is surrounded by high walls and consists of a shrine on a high podium with a pronaos (a type of entrance hall) and a narrow, rectangular cella in which were kept the sacred images, symbols and instruments used in the cult of Isis. The main altar is to be found at the side of

The Temple of Isis

Via Temple of Isis

the steps. In the south-eastern corner of the peristyle there is a small temple decorated with reliefs in stucco-work, which leads to an underground passage where the sacred water of the Nile was kept. On the opposite side, another covered altar contained the ashes and remains of a sacrifice. Behind the temple is a large room which was used as a meeting-room for the initiates of Isis.

57. SAMNITE PALAESTRA
This is also called the small palaestra to distinguish it from the large one near the Amphitheatre. The severe and delicate line of its Doric portico and its character remind us of the palaestras and habits of Greek associations. It was used for training by the noblest and richest young men of Pompeii. It developed in a small rectangular area, surrounded by a peristyle, with two entrances and a few rooms on the western side.

Along the southern side, on the base leaning against one of the columns, was the statue of Doriforo (now in the Museum of Naples), one of the best-known copies of the celebrated masterpiece. In front of the base there is an altar for offerings. Behind the base, the surviving gardens clearly show that young men used to climb up and place wreaths and crowns on the marble "simulacrum" which was a symbol of youth and strength.

58. TRIANGULAR FORUM

The main feature of the Triangular Forum is that it was built on top of a lava mass with steep sides, so that there was a drop to the plain. From here it was possible to enjoy a superb view of the sea. The main entrance is to the north, where the Propylaca (entrance portico leading to the complex) looks onto Via del Tempio di Iside (street of the Temple of Iside). Due to the irregular shape of the sacred area, the northern entrance, which corrisponds to the upper angle of a triangle, is not very large. It is proceeded by a portico with six Ionic columns and two Ionic half columns in tuff, with an architrave in tuff too. In the wall behind the colonnade, there are two doors, one small, the other larger. In front of the Propylaca colonnade there is a fountain.

After this there is the sacred area, surrounded on three sides by a portico of Doric columns and an architrave. These were divided into two parts, the upper one being composed of metopes and triglyphs (decorative parts of the wall). The columns, in tuff, are much more slender than those of the Forum. They did not, in fact, have to support a second order of columns. In front of the main façade of the the temple, on the south-eastern side, there is a strange building. It is a rectangular enclosure with the opening facing the temple, inside which there is another walled enclosure, this time lower, again facing the temple. It could possibly be the tomb of the founder of Pompeii who was later worshipped as a hero. In front of the temple, towards the right-hand corner, there are three altars built of blocks of tuff. Not far from these three altars there is a round building composed of seven Doric columns in tuff with trabeation (decorations). Inside the colonnade there is a well, cut out of the lava, similar to the one in front of Porta Vesuvius.

The Triangular Forum

The Large Theatre, still used today for entertainment purposes

59. LARGE THEATRE

The Large Theatre was built in a natural space at the top of
the hill. The seating for the public (cavea) was in the form
of a large horse-shoe, and the stage was situated at the
open end. The space between the cavea and the stage was
called the "orchestra". The cavea was divided into three
sections. Next to the "orchestra" are four large steps (ima
cavea), used by the musicians and the most important
people of the city. Behind are twenty rows of stone seats
(media cavea), which were like enormous steps about 40
cms. high and 65-70 cms. wide. Unfortunately only a few
fragments of these seats remaim. On one there is still the
number of the seat, and from this we know that each per-
son was allowed 40 cms. The media cavea is divided into
seven sections. This central zone also contains a corridor
which leads to the seven sections. Above this corridor
there are another four rows of seats (summa cavea). All the
seats were protected by a wall, on the top of which there
were spaces for wooden poles. It these were used to hold
up an enormous cloth canopy (velarium) which was attached to the top of the stage and used to protect the spectators from the sun and the wind. During the intervals the
spectators were sometimes sprinkled with perfumed wa-
ters. When these sprinklings were to take place, warnings
were given in the programmes.
The whole theatre is built in "opera incerta", even though
the surviving structure is of three different phases. Only
the stage is in "opera laterizia" and it was entirely rebuilt

after the earthquake of 62 A.D. The restoration was undertaken by Marcus Primus, who was almost certainly a freedman. This was quite common in Roman times, when architects were often slaves or descendents of slaves, since building monuments was considered degrading for a free man.

60. ARCADED COURT OF THE GLADIATORS

According to the thesis of the architect Vitruvio, every theatre provided the spectators with a large portico where they could walk during the performances, which were often very long. In Italy the use of these porticoes was inspired by Greek or Hellenistic models. However, in this case too, the portico of Pompeii, which is very well preserved, is one of the oldest examples of its kind, followed only later by the luxurious porticoes of Pompey's theatre in Rome. The portico at Pompeii is quadrangular, surrounded by 74 Doric columns in tuff stucco-work. The main entrance is to be found at the north-eastern corner. The façade of the entrance-hall has three Ionic columns in line with the columns to the east of the small courtyard behind the stage of the Large Theatre. In the north-eastern corner there is an elegant stairway which leads directly to the Triangular Forum. After 62 A.D. the Arcaded Court was changed into a barracks for gladiators. In at least ten rooms excavators found gladiators' weapons, some of which were particularly splendid, intended without a doubt to be used on parade. The helmets, with the top part folded back like modern German helmets, are typical. They also had moveable visors which left only the eyes

The Arcaded Court of the Gladiators

unprotected, and these were then covered by a metal network. The helmets, the hilts of the swords and the leg coverings are all richly decorated with scenes of Greek mythology. In two of the rooms eighteen skeletons were found, among which was a woman richly adorned with jewels.

61. ODEON (OR SMALL THEATRE)
The Odeon Theatre, also called the Small Theatre, was used for musical performances which needed a smaller, covered building, to avoid sound dispersal. It is next to the Large Theatre, forming an almost complex. Although the Odeon was built during the time of Silla, it must have been planned during the Samnite age because, from an urban pont of view, it forms a single unit together with the Large Theatre and the Arcaded Court. Its design was almost certainly inspired by a similar building which already existed in Neapolis, which was already famous for its plays and music. The building is in "opera reticolata" and "opera incerta". It has been dated from the age of Silla because up to the last century there were still traces of frescoes of the Second Style on the the walls at the front of the stage, showing that it was before Caesar.
The "ima cavea" is composed of four rows of relatively large steps on which were placed the seats (bisellie) for the decurions. At the back of the "ima cavea" is a balustrade behind which runs a passage leading to the upper steps of the "media cavea", which is divided into five wedges.

The Small Theatre

Via Stabiana

62. VIA STABIANA

The deep ruts in the huge blocks of limenstone are evidence of the intense traffic on this important road which connected the heart of Pompeii with the port, and with important citizens who lived south of the gulf. At the end of the road there was a gate with the same name.

63. PORTA DI STABIA

Porta di Stabia is the oldest preserved gate of Pompeii. On both sides of the gate there were stairways which allowed access to the path for the patrols. The double order wall flanking the gate was built using the same system as for Porta di Nola. Towards the west the external walls are built of limestone in "opera quadrata", followed by rebuilding in "opera incerta" in pre-Silla age. These walls. although they are now hidden by houses of the Imperial age, reach Porta Marina.

The Fountain where Via dell'Abbondanza crosses with Via Stabiana

64. HOUSE OF THE CITHARIST

We are in front of a large complex with three entrances, created by the union of two houses in the first century B.C. (period of the Second Style) and so containing two atria and three peristyles. The lower part, opening onto Via Stabiana, is the oldest, and has a Tuscan atrium of the Calcareous age and two peristyles added in the age of tuff, in the place of older houses knocked down to make room for these peristyles. The older part of the house was connected to the newer by means of a brick staircase between the peristyles. The building takes its name from a small bronze statue of "Apollo the Citharist" found in a peristyle and now in the National Museum. In the central peristyle, small animals, used as fountains and water sprays are to be found around the semicircular marble-covered pool. Among these is the famous group of wild boars being bitten by two hunting dogs, a racing lion, an escaping deer and a serpent, all now in the National Museum of Naples.

65. HOUSE OF THE MENANDER

An important and elegant dwelling, it was so-called because of a painting of the Greek poet Menander. It is also famous for the rich treasure found in 1930, belonging to Quintos Poppeus, a relative of Poppaea, Nero's wife. The pillars at the entrance are surmounted by two Corinthian capitals in tuff. The inside of the atrium is richly decorated in the Fourth Style with landscapes and hunting scenes, while in the right-hand corner there is a small Lararium in the form of a temple. To the left, in an exedra there is a painting showing episodes from the fall of Troy. The peristyle is grandiose, with stucco-work columns, the lower parts of which are painted red and black. Two noble rooms (oeci) open onto one side, the right-hand one being noted for its decoration: a green background and a frieze showing Centaurs and Leucippids. At the centre of the floor there is a fine mosaic of the Nile. From the eastern ambulacrum (passage for walking) opens the large triclinium, with other small rooms, all containing frescoes too. Behind these rooms are the servants' quarters. The back of the ambulacrum is composed of rectangular exedrae and apsed exedrae, all richly decorated with hunting scenes with Artemis and Atteone, and theatrical masks between figures of theatrical poets. Well preserved is the portrait of the Greek poet Menander who is seated and holding a "volumen" (book) in his hand on which is written the title of one of his plays.

The name of the poet appears on the hem of his cloak. Along the ambulacrum to the west there is the small but elegant bathroom, the entrance to which is almost hidden. The calidarium is admirably preserved and its paintings, mosaic and stucco-work are noteworthy.

The House of the Menander

66. HOUSE OF THE LOVERS

This is a well-preserved house, small but pretty. The house takes its name from a graffito in a picture found in the ambulacrum of the peristyle: "Amantes ut apes vitam mellitam exigent!" that is "Lovers, like bees, make life as sweet as honey!" From the beautifully decorated atrium, one passes into the peristyle with two rows of columns onto which faces a large triclinium with a vaulted roof and paintings showing "Bacchus and Ariadne" and "Dido abandoned".

67. HOUSE OF LUCIUS CEIUS SECUNDUS

The beautiful original façade, which imitated "opera quadrata" in stone, and the cornice reconstructed with materials taken from the excavation, are still preserved intact. In the vestibule, the plaster cast of the first and second doors are in their original places, and the ceiling has been rebuilt. An almost intact stairway leading to the upper floor has been discovered in the tetrastyle atrium, and to the left there is the cast of a cupboard in which a razor was found. Behind the atrium there is a small peristyle whose walls are decorated with large paintings showing wild beasts in liberty and Egyptian landscapes containing Africans and pygmies.

68. HOUSE OF THE CRYPTOPORTICUS

The atrium and peristyle are not very well preserved, but the cryptoporticus, reached by a stairway, is very interesting. Another stairway gave access to the neighbouring House of the Lararium before it was sold. The new owner, probably a wine merchant, was changing two wings of the cryptoporticus into a warehouse. In the third wing there are still traces of decorations in the Second Style: a circular vault with stuccoes and panels of floral designs and walls divided by female herms holding up a frieze of scenes from the Iliad. In the beautiful dining-room, also in the Second Style, there are caryatids painted in red which support a frieze of ritual pictures and still lifes. In the garden of the house were found the "bodies" of the inhabitants. At the moment of the eruption they had sheltered in the cryptoporticus and tried to escape through a type of sky-light. They were suffocated in the fall of the ash, however, and the casts of their bodies are to be seen in the north wing of the crypt.

69. FULLONICA OF STEPHANUS

This laundry, excavated in 1911 and still well-preserved, is the only one of the four laundries of the last period of Pompeii, almost completely rebuilt. The others were adapted as well as possible in older houses. The entrance here is very large, as is fit for a shop, to allow for the coming and going of the customers. When the eruption took

The Fullonica (Laundry) of Stephanus in Via dell'Abbondanza

place the vertical wooden door was closed on the outside with a large chain. Only the single door which was hinged was found open, because the hinge was broken, and in the office behind there was a skeleton with a sum of money in gold, silver and bronze of the value of 1089. 5 sesterces. The laundries had a dual purpose. They were used to finish the material, before it was cut, by washing out dirt absorbed during the weaving process, and also for normal washing and cleaning of clothes. The Romans had a particular system for washing their white tunics. In order to deliver the clothes, the customer had to pass through a room in which there was a press (torcular or pressorium), to the left of the entrance, and also the atrium behind. The impluvium was transformed into a tub with shelves, probably used for washing the more delicate clothes. In the compluvium there was a sky-light in the flat roof. This is the only example of an atrium with a flat roof preserved in Pompeii. It is important since it offered the advantage of a large terrace for hanging out the washing. Behind the peristyle three other tubs were built (lacus), in communication due to holes in the walls and sloping floors, and emptied with pails and syphons. There were also five oval tubs for trampling (lacunae fullonicae), three to the left, with a round vessel for the urine, and two to the right with another vessel of the same type. Along the tubs are elevated passages for the workers who could enter the tubs by means of steps. In the "trampling tubs" the clothers were trampled underfoot in a mixture of water and soda or other alkaline substances, often human or animal urine (that of camels was very precious). The human urine, from the time of the wise Vespasian, was collected in "vespasiani" (public toilets) or even in simple amphorae placed in factories for the collection of the urine. The fullatores were taxed for using urine in the same way that water was taxed. Even before the time of Vespasian the owners of the laundries invited passers-by to urinate into vessels placed in the streets or near the entrances for this purpose. Hardened by the urine, the cloth was then treated with clay, the best of which was imported from the island of Kimolos, one of the Cyclades in the Aegean Sea or with "terra umbrica", dark-coloured earth, that came from Sardinia being considered of inferior quality. It was then battered to condense the weft, washed again to rinse off the various substances used and to shrink the material, and finally carded with "aena", combing-cards made of vegetable thorns or porcupine quills, to ease the shearing. The white materials, and those dyed twice, were given a special sulphur treatment to make them shinier. They were then hardened with "creta cimolia" or "terra umbrica", or with pumice if they were white, and finally brushed, combed, dampened and ironed under the press. A staircase leads to the terrace found above the peristyle and atlium, where there was air and wind for drying and bleaching in the sun.

70. HOUSE OF THE LARARIUM
At the time of the eruption this house was being modernized. To the right of the tablinum is a small room containing an unusually shaped Lararium. It is surrounded by a small canal with a podium and a sloping roofed niche, all painted with a red backgrond.

71. WORKSHOP OF VERECUNDUS
This was one of the most typical of the Pompeii factories where dress materials and felt objects were produced and clothes were manufactured. The façade is very interesting because the roof juts out over it. At the sides of the entrance there were four paintings, two of which were dedicated to the gods which protected the factory, "Mercury and Venus of Pompeii in a chariot drawn by four elephants" and to the right are scenes of the factory and selling over the counter.

72. THERMOPOLIUM OF ASELLINA
The thermopolium (refreshment room) of Asellina is to be found on Via dell'Abbondanza, with its hot and cold drinks, ready-cooked food, and alcoves on the upper floor. The excavation has left all the shop furnishings in their original places; wine urns, a funnel, the phallic oil-lamp which illuminated the counter and kept the evil-eye away and even a pot on the fire. Certain graffiti on the walls sug-

The House of the Lararium: two interior views

gest that as well as giving refreshment, Asellina offered the lively company of young girls. Since Pompeii was a port, and customers came from all parts of the Mediterranean, the owner had also obtained foreign girls, so that it was pleasant for a foreigner to enter this international tavern where he could find friendly fellow countrymen and women.

Graffiti next to the Thermopolium of Asellina

73. HOUSE OF PAQUIUS PROCULUS

A mosaic in the form of a carpet covers the entire floor of the vestibulum, atrium and peristyle. In the vestibulum there is a chained dog, in the atrium and tablinum on a white background stand out pictures with figures of animals and people.

The House of Paquius Proculus

The main rooms of the house are to be found around a peristyle with garden and an open-air triclinium. In one of the rooms off the peristyle there is a small humorous mosaic: a mule falling under the weight of a silenus and two men at its sides trying to help it, one pulling its ears and the other its tail.

74. HOUSE OF THE PRIEST AMANDUS
In the fauces of the entrance is the partial cast of a human body, the only one remaining of people, adults, women and children who crowded together desperately, anxious to escape into the street, and instead suffocated to death. On the walls to the right of the fauces there is a rough painting of pre-Roman age, showing a fight, probably during the funeral games. Inside the house is a noteworthy triclinium with decorations in the Third Style, to the right of the atrium.

75. HOUSE OF THE EPHEBE
Three doors gave access to this house which was probably obtained from the joining of neighbouring houses. It represents the type of dwelling of a merchant who had become rich through business in the last few years of the city. Here the bronze statue of the Ephebe, used as a lampshade, was found in the convivial dining-room of the garden.

76. HOUSE OF THE ORCHARD
On the walls of two of the cubicles of the house there is an interesting naturalistic painting. It is on a blue and black background and depicts different fruit-trees: fig, plum, pear, sorb-apple, cherry and lemon, which were considered a rarity in Campania in the first century B.C.
Further along Via dell'Abbondanza, to the left, there is the House of Trebius Valens which allows us to catch a glimpse of an unusual checkered design painted on the back wall of the peristyle and also a triclinium under a bower and amid drops of water.

77. HOUSE OF TREBIUS VALENS
At one time the exterior of this house attracted attention because it seems to have been used for public notices, the plaster being covered in a great many mural inscriptions (now destroyed). There were electoral programmes of the owner of the house and three advertisements for public spectacles in the amphitheatre with the lists of the names of the couples of gladiators and the names of the champions but without the useful notice that the amphitheatre would have had the canopy for protection from the sun and heat. The interior of the house has an interesting effect, above all thanks to the unusual checkered design on the back wall of the peristyle. There is also a triclinium under an arbour with twelve water spouts, an elegant bed-

The House of Trebius Valens

room in the Second Style, a living room with a black background and a small private bathroom behind the kitchen.

78. SCHOLA ARMATURARUM

This is a large room, closed by a transenna, which was probably used as the centre of a military association. All the pictoial decorations are inspired by military designs: on the outside are two large trophies of war. On the internal pillars are stylized chandeliers with military emblems at the top. Along the northern and eastern walls (internal), there are signs of wooden cabinets which were probably used for the weapons, since the transenna was too low to hold them.

79. HOUSE OF THE MORALIST

So-called because of the three rules painted in the triclinium. On the three walls of the room are written three precepts which the owner, Epidius Hymenaeus, wanted his guests to observe. They were painted on a black background, but one was unfortunately destroyed during the bombings in 1943.
"Abluat unda pedes, puer et detergeat udos.
Mappa torum velet, lintea nostra cave".
The servant shall wash and dry the feet of the guest;
a cloth must protect the cushions and the linen must be well cared for.
"Lascivos vultus et blandos auper ocellos
coniuge ab alternius: sibi tibi in ore puder".
Abandon lascivious looks and do not cast sweet glances at

the women of others; be chaste in speech.
"(Utere blandit) iis, odiosaque iugge differ
si potes, a ut gressus ad tua tecta refer".
Abstain from anger if possible, if not return to your own
home.

80. HOUSE OF LOREIUS TIBERTINUS

Almost opposite, between two shops, there is the enormous portal, with the casts of the doors decorated with metal knobs, which leads into the house of Loreius Tibertinus, a priest of the goddess Isis.
Worth noting is the beautiful landscaping effect at the back of the house, including the loggia, the garden on two different levels and the water play. It is, in fact, the house of the priest of Isis where, during the sacred holidays, the overflowing of the Nile was reproduced, and finished up with a banquet in the triclinium in front of the sacred sacellum (small altar). The arched loggia, which was raised above the level of the garden and protected by a pergola had a canal running through it.
In the centre there was a temple through which the water gushed into the forementioned canal and crossed the entire garden, interrupted by another temple. The most luxurious rooms face this loggia; to the east there is a triclinium (dining-room) with scenes from the Iliad, Latin inscriptions and fragments of an episode of the myth of Hercules. To the west the loggia ends with a room decorated with white panels on which are to be found various figures and

The House of Loreius Tibertinus

The House of Loreius Tibertinus

medallions. Among the figures is a priest of Isis which is probably the owner of the house.

81. HOUSE OF VENUS

The atrium was badly damaged during the bombings in 1943, but the paintings of the peristyle still retain their freshness.

The nude Venus, sailing on a seashell, on the rear wall of the peristyle is painted in a clumsy way, but when seen from a distance, gives a good impression. She has a fan in her right hand, while her left is holding her veil, which is blowing in the wind. Her hairstyle shows typical curls and she is wearing gold jewellery; a tiara, a necklace and bracelets on her wrists and ankles.

The decorative panels, as usual, take no notice of the architecture. The decorators rarely adhered to rules of symmetry in their schemes, and ignored the elements that were foreign to their paintings.

82. HOUSE OF JULIA FELIX

After the House of Venus is the House of Julia Felix, as revealed by a notice attached to the outside wall which is now in the Museum of Naples. We do not know why this relatively rich woman, to judge by her property, was forced to rent most of her beautiful dwelling and private baths. Perhaps it was due to the economic crisis through which the city passed in the years between the earthquake and the eruption. The house itself occupies less than half the block, the rest being an orchard. The whole of the complex (praedium) consisted of: the house of the owner, a private bath, shops with living quarters and an area to rent on the western side. Through a vestibulum leading off Via dell'Abbondanza there was a garden with a fish-pond with small bridges and niches for feeding the fish. There is also an elegant portico of slim, white pillars to the west, with pillars in stucco-work surrounding the southern and eastern sides. On the back wall there are rectangular and semi-circular niches. Beneath the western portico, at the centre, there is a triclinium with marble couches, and at

The House of Venus

The House of Julia Felix

the far wall, a fountain with steps leading up to it, from which water gushed. Along the southern wall, around a small atrium, there is the actual dwelling, with an entrance from the street to the west. Kitchen and servants' rooms were to the west, while to the east were the living rooms which opened onto the orchard and garden. The private baths had a main entrance from Via dell'Abbondanza by means of an elegant doorway composed of semi-columns, which gave way to a portico also used as a vestibulum with chairs for waiting. The actual baths were composed of a dressing-room, tepidarium, calidarium and laconicum. The heating system of the three rooms, with raised floors and hollow walls, is almost perfect. From the vestibulum or from the dressing-room it was possible to reach an open space with a swimming-pool and gymnasium. The tabernae, although they had access to the main street, were also in direct communication with the baths, and contained internal rooms as dining-rooms to satisfy the tastes of their rich clients. The tabernae also contained mezzanines used as storerooms or sleeping-quarters for the slaves. On the western side there was an area for rent with living-quarters on the top floors, which were reached by means of stairways from the ground floors.

83. AMPHITHEATRE
This was built in 80 B.C. by the builders of the Small Theatre, and is to be considered the oldest known amphitheatre.

The building is situated at the extreme east of the city, leaning against the walls which used the earth dug out of the centre to support steps.

For this reason the arena is at a lower level than the surrounding area and there are no underground passages. Two main entrances along the longest axis led into the arena itself and to the lower seating level. The upper levels were reached by external stairways with two ramps. Facing the square in front of the building there is a large embanked wall built of dry-stone, with large stone arches.

Let us now see how the spectators entered the amphitheatre. A vaulted gallery ran under the end seats of the "media cavea" (middle seating area).

This gallery, also known as a crypt, had a double function of supporting the external part of the embankment, and of allowing an orderly flow of people to the seats. There was also a central interruption to prevent the crowds of people from heading towards the same opening. The crypt is to be reached by means of four corridors, one to the north and three to the west, all of which are sloping. The two passages at the extreme ends lead directly into the arena. Since these were also used for carts and carriages, they are well-paved with irregular blocks of basalt. The south-western corridor bends in order to reach the arena. Immediately to the right of the entrance, after the stairway, one arrives at the surrounding wall, in which it was impossible to create openings.

A complete view of the Amphitheatre

All the passages and the crypt, vaulted and built in "opera cementizia", were restored after the earthquake of 62 A.D. Access to the outside of the Amphitheatre is under the subterranean arcade of the double flighted stairway on the western side. The presence of small stairways in the corridor, almost on a level with the crypt leads us to believe that this passage was possibly used by the most eminent magistrates of the city in order to reach the seats of honour which must have been situated on a platform resting on the crypt.

The outlet to the arena was probably used by the victors to reach the platform and receive their prizes. Continuing along the crypt, one returns to the entrance to the arena. Before arriving at the entrances, both to the north and to the south, there are two small rooms most likely used as "spogliarii", where wounds were treated and where the bodies of dead gladiators were brought. The arena was entered, therefore, through a large portal in cut stone with semi-circular arches, pillars ending in simple capitals, cornices, friezes and collarino (decorative elements). From the centre of the arena it is possible to gain a clear impression of the form of the Amphitheatre.

It is to be noted that the elliptical shape is not regular, due to pre-existing ramparts which have altered the form of the ellipse to the east.

The seating area is divided into three main zones, using dividing barriers in accurately cut blocks of tuff. The "ima cavea" (lower seating area), is divided into six sections, using brick transennae (barriers). Since the "ima cavea" was reserved for the most important people of the city, it seems probable that the sections corresponded to a strict class distinction. The "media cavea" (middle) and "summa cavea" (upper) are divided by intermediate stairways into twenty wedges, each of which, in the "summa cavea" is subdivided by another stairway.

The Amphitheatre also had a velarium (large canopy) to protect the spectators from the excessive heat of the sun. From ancient sources we also know these canopies were made. That of the colosseum, for example, was of the finest linen, dark blue with stars on it. At the centre of the canopy was the portrait of the Emperor. The canopy of the Amphitheatre of Pompeii was certainly not as fine, but it was probably of linen.

The passion of the Italic peoples for gladiator spectacles was great, on a level with football nowadays.

84. LARGE PALAESTRA

The Palaestra is to be found next to the Amphitheatre with which it shares a huge square. This position was probably chosen for the construction of the building because it is without housing. Apart from this, the large houses to the north of the Palaestra have enormous gardens to the rear,

The Large Palaestra

which would have been impossible if the area had been densely populated.

The Large Palaestra had a dual purpose. On the one hand Pompeii lacked a large building to be used as a gymnasium by the young people, who were evidently forced to use the palaestra in the Stabian Baths. The so-called Samnite Palaestra, was very small, and apart from being used by a military corporation, was totally inadequate. On the other hand, in the Augustan age the Emperor decided to reorganize the young people in actual associations (collegia iuvenum).

The gymnasiums which were created during this period had, therefore, an important function; that of imperial propoganda. In this way, Augustan ideals were easily accepted by the young people who were politically inexperienced. This explains the creation of such a palaestra, rectangular (about 141 metres x 107 metres), with an extremely wide road to the north, flanked by enormous plane-trees, containing a huge swimming-pool (34.35 metres x 22.25 metres). It is enclosed by a high wall, originally battlemented, built in "opera incerta", with ten large entrances to the east, north and west. The southern side rests on the embankment of the wall. The original walls of the Augustan building were in "opera incerta", formed of chips of lava from Vesuvius. The whole of the northern wall, which fell during the earthquake of 62 A.D. and which is still to be seen at the base of the new wall (built recently), shows a similar construction technique. The doors to the east and the west are in "opera laterizia" with ample quadrangular door-spaces surmounted by an arch. The internal and external facings are decorated with semi-columns, architraves and gables.

The capital is simply formed of cincture and double tiles. Internally the enclosure is surrounded on three sides by a portico, composed of 35 columns on the northern and southern sides and of 48 columns on the western side.

It was possible to reach the slightly lower level of the Palaestra by means of four small flights of steps in the four corners and a larger flight in the centre of the western side. At the centre of the Palaestra is the swimming-pool (natatio), extremely large, like modern-day pools. It was built sloping from a minimum of one metre to a maximum of 2.60 metres. Water entered from a "castellum" (water cistern) found at the entrance to the road passing the western side of the House of Loreius Tiburtinus.

As in the case of all the drainage systems of the area, however, the pipes had not been connected.

85. PORTA NOCERA

Porta Nocera shows a remarkable resemblance to Porta di Nola and Porta Stabia. In this case too, from the gate of the city to a vaulted space where the actual gate was situated, there is a corridor with two ramparts at the ends. The gate is flanked lengthways by a double-ordered citywall,

The Necropolis of Porta Nocera

on which can still be seen traces of steps on the south-eastern side.

Inside the double-ordered citywalls can be noted the buttresses. The inner order is composed of blocks of limestone and tuff on which are sometimes to be found Oscan markings. Another wall, completely built of limestone, leans against this wall, as can be seen from the shape of the earth on the western side.

The external city walls, composed of limestone blocks, are still well-preserved.

86. NECROPOLIS OF PORTA NOCERA

Pompeii had, like every other ancient city, a necropolis outside every gate. Via Nuceria runs from west to west, and is crossed, near the gate, by another road heading south. Today this road comes to a stop after a few metres, beside the embankment of Via Nazionale. At the cross-roads, about a hundred steps from the Gate, there is the boundary-stone, which reminds us here, as at Porta Ercolano and Porta Vesuvius, of the way that Suedio Clemente, an imperial commissioner, claimed land from private owners to give to the colony.

The tombs to the west and east of the cross-roads are in four forms. They are either composed of a pedestal with an additional "ara" (small altar) or are burial rooms with niches and barrel-vaults, or true mausoleums of one or two floors or tabernacles on a high pedestal. Marked by

On this and following pages: casts obtained by pouring plaster into the spaces left by the decomposed bodies

inscriptions and often by funeral stautes in marble or in tuff, they are also closed in the surrounding walls or protected by stones which limited the area.

The tombs were probably built during the last republican period or during the Imperial age (Julius-Claudius).

On some of the stucco walls of the tombs which faced the public roads, are to be found electoral inscriptions. To the west of the cross-roads is a large group of burial monuments, following a southerly line. In this area is the Tomb of Eumachia. Continuing eastwards along the northern boundary we come to a tomb with steps surmounted by an altar without inscriptions. Following this there is a chamber tomb belonging to the governor L. Celluis (a military magistrate elected by the people), with fine stucco-work panels, and other chamber tombs with inscriptions relating to the gladiators of Pompeii and Nocera.

On the opposite side of the street is the large circular mausoleum which a woman, Veia Barchilla, built for herself and her husband, N. Agrestinus Equitius Pulcher. She was rich and far-sighted in providing her dearly beloved husband with such a luxurious tomb.

In 59 A.D., the same year that Nero killed his mother, Agrippina, there was a fight in the Amphitheatre between Pompeians and Nocerians, which resulted in a massacre. This fact caused a sensation and even Tacitus spoke about it in his "Annals" as follows:

"In that time there was a fierce massacre between men from Pompeii and from Nocera. It originated from a futile reason to do with the gladiators' games organized by Livineis Regolo who had been banished from the Senate. At first they just exchanged provincial insults, then went on to stone throwing and finally resorted to weapons, prevailing the inhabitants of Pompeii, in front of whom the spectacle took place".

"Many men of Nocera were taken home badly injured and others lost their lives. Nero referred the fact to the Senate which passed it on to the consuls. When it returned to the Senate it was decided to ban all similar spectacles for ten years: those associations which were formed against these laws were ordered to disband and those that had provoked the massacre were sent into exile".

87. GARDEN OF THE FUGITIVES

A small portico was used as a vestibulum of this well-built house which, during the last years of the city, had been converted into a country-house for the production of wine and the cultivation of the vast orchard which reached the embankment of the city walls.

It was in this orchard in 1961, that the impressions of thirteen victims were found in the laver of ashes. They had remained in the house during the fall of lapilli and then tried to escape under the ashes.

They suffocated to death, however, and fell one after the other in their family groups; adults, young people and children. The casts taken, and which are shown in the same order as they were found, are one of the most dramatic examples of the death which overtook Pompeii and her people.

Southern view of Pompeii

One of the numerous fountains to be found while walking along the streets of Pompeii

88. VILLA OF THE MYSTERIES

The actual entrance is through a small portico leading into a semi-circular room which opens onto an uncovered terrace. This is not the original ancient entrance, which is on the other side of the Villa, still covered in volcanic material. The Villa of the Mysteries is a typical example of a luxurious house containing a farm annex. It is situated on quite a steep slope, with all parts facing the sea, resting on an artificial embankment under which is the cryptoporticus, used as a cellar.

The main rooms of the house revolve around the atrium, which included a cubicle, oeci (type of dining-room), a tablinum and an exedra with semi-circular windows, and an area of house facilities around a peristyle, including a tetrastyle atrium with a bathroom. Besides this there is also

The Villa of Mysteries: on the opposite page, small Satyr and figure in flight (cycle of frescoes dedicated to the Dionysiac mysteries); on this page, external view of the Villa

85

The Villa of Mysteries: the internal courtyard; above and on the opposite page, a "trompe l'oeil" decorated room, in the Second style

a courtyard with the kitchens, oven and servants' quarters and a farm area with room for the manager and for the farm equipment.

The villa is richly decorated, one of the paintings being a cycle of enormous figures possibly representing the initiation of a bride into the Dionysiac mysteries. In the so-called Room of the Large Painting there is a cycle of frescoes covering all the walls which are the successive stages of a single ceremony: a young man reads the ritual under the guidance of a seated woman, another woman follows closely and a young woman with a tray of offerings makes to the right.

A group of women assist at a sacrificial ceremony; an old Silenus sings and plays while a young woman offers her breast to a fawn. A woman terrified by the sacred vision, retreats: an old Silenus offers a young Satyr to drink while another young man holds up a theatrical mask.

Villa of Mysteries, frescoes dedicated to the Dionysiac cerimonies: on the previous pages, the decorated hall and scenes from the cycle depicting a seated matron, a boy reading the ritual, and a back view of a seated sacrificer; on the opposite page, reading of the rites and uncovering of the Dionysiac phallus; above, a Silenus offering a drink to a small Satyr

The Marriage of Dionysus and Ariadne; a young woman, kneeling, seems to be uncovering a sacred object from a red cover.

A winged figure holds up a whip to strike a terrified young woman who tries to hide in the lap of her companion; after she is purified by the act of the winged demon she gets up and dances nude estatically.

Toilet of a bride before the rite: finally, in a corner, there is the figure of a seated woman, covered in a mantle. She is already a bride, perhaps a priestess of the god and is watching the ritual.

On this and following page, three views of the Villa
of Diomedes

89. VILLA OF DIOMEDES

This splendid suburban villa is about a kilometre from
Porta Ercolano. It is a magnificent dwelling and attracted
interest when when it came to light in 1771-74 because of
the discovery of eighteen skeletons in an underground portico. Very little of the rich mural decorations remains, only
a few paintings being preserved in the Archaeological
Museum of Naples. All the same, the villa is interesting for
its layout. The complex faces west and has two floors. The
house is centred around the atrium-peristyle and is linked
to the large garden which is on a lower level. Above the
covered arcades which surrounded the whole of the "viridarium" (garden), there was a solarium or sun terrace and
an "ambulatorio" where open-air walks could be taken. At
the ends there were two covered towers from which the
sea-view could be enjoyed. Under the covered arcade ran
a large gallery or cryptoporticus which was being
trasformed into a cellar, probably for the amphorae of
wine, during the last years. These alterations were begun
by the last owner, almost certainly an important wine merchant.

To the left, in a triangular area between the peristyle and the road there is the bathing area with a kitchen and a water reservoir. In the tepidarium the window was closed with four panes of glass.
Leading off from the peristyle there was a semi-circular cubicle with an alcove, a wash-basin and servants' rooms with alcoves too.

ALPHABETIC INDEX

Restaurant
Self-Service - Bar - Pizzeria
SUISSE

Open all day
6.00 a.m. - 7.00 p.m.
Hot and cold food

*T*o complete your visit to
Pompeii,
take advantage of the
services offered by the
"Suisse" Restaurant

Regional specialities

Closed on Mondays
Tel. 081/8610185 - Fax 081/5369997